TOPIC SECTION "A"

Introduction to Real Estate

Skills of a Real Estate Agent

Introduction to Real Estate

Real Estate is a sector that many professionals (Real Estate Agents, Brokers, Developers, Builders) take action on, however few understand it in depth. According to several entrepreneurs I have personally talked to in individual sessions, in the field of Business Coaching and Real Estate (most recently with Bartek who owns a real estate agency in France), to be considered a successful Real Estate Agent / Broker you must have the following skills:

SKILLS

1.   **Manage properly time.** As I mention in Time Management seminars where I teach, the successful person is not the one who will make 2 sales, having gone to 50 appointments, but the one who will make 1 sale in 10 appointments. This naturally involves understanding, updating, specific and key questions that need to be told to customers in order to save time and not just waste your time, in which time you could have made 2 sales instead of 1.

2.   Remember that **each day you spend you have one less to spend**, so ask the right questions to the customer to know exactly what he / she is asking for (Specific Questions).

3.   **Invest in Marketing**. In smart media promotions, on the web and keep customer lists. It helps keep your lists updated and communication.

SKILLS

1.   **Have an investment plan-strategy** and not wake up every morning and ask "what is going on today?" That way, it is sure you and your affiliates to say goodbye to your interest to the subject if you find that things "don't move 'as you wish.

2.   Be polite and not distant. Be able to break the ice inside yourself first so you can be more spontaneous and accessible to customers.

3.   To cover the needs of the customer means learning to listen! So active listening! Never sell what you want to give, but sell what the customer wants and needs!

4.   Keep be trained in the real estate sector and learn what's new on the market. Be aware!

SKILLS

1.   Keep in touch with customers. Not only when you want to sell them, but also after a successful sale! It's really incredible when I hear Business Owners who have sold enough apartments or expensive real estate to a customer, after a while they can't even remember his name! Communication and contact are an important part of a Real Estate Agent, both on a personal level and on new horizons that open up.

2.   **Learn the art of negotiation.** Keep in mind that communication is 7% based on verbal speech and 93% on voice tone and body movements. This means that you should not limit yourself to the conversation alone, but you should focus on strategic points for the customer (voice tone, eye movements, posture, etc.), especially at negotiation time!

3.   **Be yourself**. No one can do it better!

SKILLS

All start with your self-talk, which leads to self-sabotage. This is a big deal because your attitude is actually your reality. **How you see the world and what this bubble in your mind tells you.** That's where all start, and that comes from your attitude. Actions get results and depend on what kind of results you have.

When you have restrictive beliefs in your mind, such as "I am not capable", "I will not make money", "I can not do it", then the action you take in will not have the intensity and power. Reduced action will therefore not deliver the expected results, so your restrictive beliefs will be further strengthened: "You saw, I told them I couldn't", "I knew I wouldn't do it" ... and so you spend yourselves on thoughts.

BELIEFS = THOUGHTS = ACTS = UNEXPECTED RESULTS = BELIEFS REINFORCEMENTS = EVEN MORE OMINUS THOUGHTS = WORSE RESULTS and a vicious circle is created

To clear your mind and body, we will refer some techniques to relax or strengthen yourself:

Deepak Chopra taught me that there is a connection between our body and our mind. If we move our body in a strong way, it directly affects our posture and our postures will give us a positive energy, it's that simple!

RELAXATION TECHNIQUES

Here are 3 key elements to keeping calm and relaxation:

"Motion creates Emotion"

1. **Nutrition, hydration and proper breathing** are the key ingredients to getting us into action and getting the results we want!

2. **Diaphragmatic Breathing** (with inhalation, the abdomen ONLY, not the chest, inflates like a balloon, and deflates with exhalation. 6 to 7 breaths per minute is ideal, scientists say).

3. **Don't let past negative experiences become the story of your future actions**. I want you change these stories and delete their power to take the next step, both on a personal and professional level.

Real estate Coaching

Real Estate coaching is based on the principles of Life & Business Coaching.

The Real Estate coach is a "bridge"! A bridge that helps us to move from one level to another (goal). The Real Estate Coach is Encouragement, Motivation, Personal Discovery and Evolution ... All of the above is based on a single word: RELATIONSHIP!

Coaching is a Supportive Relationship, a Relationship Created (between parties), and the strategy that is followed is fundamentally aimed at discovering and becoming aware of our best selves as well as Exploring-Discovering-Improving our skills and abilities. It is a kind of personal and emotional development, personal reinforcement, and nourishing the unknown energy that we all hide within us.

RELATIONSHIP-DISCOVERY-IMPROVEMENT for PROGRESS and EVOLUTION!

Page 9

Real estate Coaching

Real Estate Coaching helps the client (Coachee):

- ☐ To develop his/her communication skills.
- ☐ To Strengthen his/her Labor and Interpersonal relationships.
- ☐ To Increase his/her confidence and productivity.
- ☐ To Become more creative.
- ☐ To Recognize and manage his/her emotions.

- ☐ To Build Self-Esteem - Capability & How to Achieve Its Goals!

- ☐ To Understand his/her needs

- ☐ To Make the changes he/she wants

- ☐ To Apply strategies and practices to accomplish his/her goals

- ☐ To Get in the action and get out of his/her comfort zone

- ☐ In practice, he/she will help him/her identify the gap between where he/she is now and where he/she wants to go and help him/her bridge that gap.

CODE OF DEONTOLOGY

Coaching: Defines Coach's collaboration with clients (Coachees) in a creative thinking process to maximize personal and professional potential and skills.

Professional relationship: Includes a contract or agreement with each party's terms and conditions

Client / Coachee: Defines the person who accepts Coaching

Sponsor: It can be a business, an organization, an institution, an entity, together with representatives or affiliates, who pays and arranges the Coaching services they wish to improve Coachee's performance. The contract must clearly state the obligations, conditions, responsibilities and rights of both the client and the sponsor, if they are not the same person.

CODE OF DEONTOLOGY

As a Real Estate Coach & Life Coach, I should:

☐ formulate accurately (orally or in writing) my coaching qualifications, qualifications, experience, training, certifications and accreditation.

☐ acknowledge and honor the efforts and contributions of others and claim ownership of only my own material. understand that violating this standard can leave me exposed to litigations by third parties.

☐ avoid any romantic or sexual relationships with clients, sponsors, students or supervisors.

☐ be vigilant to prevent the development of sexual intimacy between the aforementioned parties and do everything necessary to settle the matter or even cancel the agreement so as to provide a totally safe environment.

CODE OF DEONTOLOGY

Coach & coachee (Client) will maintain strict levels of confidentiality for all client and sponsor information unless disclosure is required by law.

☐ They must conclude a clear agreement, both with the client and with the sponsor, student, mentee, about the circumstances under which confidentiality cannot be respected (eg illegal activity, valid warrant or summons, threatened or a potential danger to himself and others, etc.) and make sure that they are consciously and freely agreed to

☐	Life Coach uses coaching tools and models to elicit helpful customer responses that will lead to solutions.

☐	It is necessary to have an overview of the whole process-sessions, in order to have a picture of the customer's improvement and if we are leading to the desired results

CODE OF DEONTOLOGY

☐	The Life Coach (or Real Estate Coach) openly discloses any conflicts of interest and leaves the whole process in case of such a conflict.

☐	clarifies roles between internal Coaches, sets boundaries and reviews conflicts of interest with stakeholders.

☐	discloses to the client or sponsor any legal compensation that he or she may receive or is required to pay to third parties to refer to that client (International Coaching Federation only).

☐	respects the client's choice to terminate the Coaching process at any time under terms of agreement and if the client no longer benefits from the relationship.

☐	encourages the Sponsor or client to terminate the Coaching relationship and be served by another Coach, Mentor, the other qualified professional.

CODE OF DEONTOLOGY

☐　　The Life Coach (or Real Estate Coach) should recognize personal issues or problems that may affect his/her performance, so he/she immediately seeks professional help, suspension or termination of coaching relationships.

☐　　Members must be healthy and capable of performing their duties as Coaches. If they are uncertain and health problems arise, they should seek professional guidance / support and, where appropriate, Coach should terminate the Coaching with the client and refer him to an alternative source of support.

☐　　Coach is also committed to developing his/her professional skills and constantly evolving.

☐　　Members develop their level of competence in Coaching services and participate in relevant and continuing training / Continuing Vocational Training

☐　　Members will be involved in supervision with a supervisor (or group supervisor) who possesses the appropriate skills and qualifications, in accordance with the requirements of each professional body and their level of certification.

TOPIC SECTION "B"

Getting Started in Real Estate

THE BEGINNING ....

To begin with, to start up a company / business, or to achieve a great sales, both professionally and personally, you should to:

☐ 1. **Commit to your goals.** This may seem obvious, but if you have the attitude that you are going to do something, that you are committed to accomplishing your goal, and not just wanting to do it, then you are much more likely to succeed. With desire, you will simply expect to come in handy situations in your life to grab them. **With commitment**, you create opportunities for **YOU**. **With Commitment**, you will do whatever it takes to succeed!

☐ 2. **Make a plan for achievement your goals**. A vague idea, like I want to do 3 or 5 or 10 home sales a month will not get you where you want to be. Make yourself a roadmap. **SPECIFIC GOALS**!

☐ 3. **Play roles**. Be ready for objections. Make a list of potential customer objections, and then spend time thinking about the answers.

☐ 4. **Reaching customers.** Talk to new people. Clients or Real Estate Agents. With the passage of time, it will help your business as well as you personally.

THE BEGINNING ....

☐ **Knowledge.** To be an up-to-date seller, you need to know what's going on in your area: What are the new properties? Which properties were sold? What are the sales? What are the prices on the market?

☐ **Personal Mentor or Coach.** You should really try to get in touch with a mentor or a Coach who can help you grow.

☐ **Attend seminars or conferences.** Take advantage of a seminar, conference or webinar on the subject of your work.

☐ **Web page.** Learn how to use SEO and embed it into whatever you can on your site as well as make sure to get promoted in the web. If you are not well-versed in SEO & specialized in internet tools, let a specialist to do it.

☐ **Positivity.** Believing in yourself also helps you accomplish your goals!

REAL ESTATE CHARACTERISTICS

As My Valuable and Award-winning Sellers & Partners have written in "Pathos Real Estate Coach" The features a Real Estate Agent should have are:

- [ ] **Politeness**
- [ ] **Good Preparation**
- [ ] **Humor**
- [ ] **Authenticity**
- [ ] **Patience ...**

The thing that comes up with most Real Estate Agents is that they have to combine all of the above with:

- [ ] **Persistence**
- [ ] **Determination**
- [ ] **Targeting**
- [ ] **Forcefulness**

QUESTIONS TO ANSWER

Take paper and pen and answer the following questions:

1. **What do I love about selling homes**? What really do I love about selling houses?

Once you understand this, the work you do will be effortless and enjoyable because you focus on the things you love!

1. What do I love about my clients and my prospects?

Don't just think about difficult clients. Take a great distance from yourself and see the situation globally. Think about what you really love about your customers and prospects. For your clients, this can be about helping them find a new home. Their lives will change. They will be happier, they will start a new life and more. You are capable of offering smiles to your customers and getting rid of their problems and worries with the right guidance.

QUESTIONS TO ANSWER

1. What do I really love about finding new customers? Think of all the people you can influence and help! As a real estate agent, you have the ability to reach thousands of people throughout your career. New acquaintances, great intensity, activities, new buildings, new clients and personalities that evolve you both professional and individual.

2. What do I do? Here, you really need to find your inner motivation and motivation that will drive you to action and enjoyment. It is up to you whether you will see a job as a chore or as a development and social contribution. "My grandmother never saw food preparation and cleaning as a chore for her children and grandchildren, but she saw it as offering smiles and satisfaction to others, so she had created her own reality. She had this motivation." What I mean by the above simulation, that what you believe you are doing, this will be your reality! I knew, for example, two Civil Servants. One believed that what he was doing was simply stamping and sinking into a chair. The other employee had an appetite for believing that he was helping people get their pensions, and he even talked to the world about having a good time. Guess who was the happiest ...

"WETHER YOU THINK YOU CAN OR YOU CAN'T EITHER WAY,

YOU ARE RIGHT"

Henry Ford

With those you associate with, you will look like ...

'You will be like those you associate with' is the title of an article I wrote for a magazine in the United Kingdom (and then published in Greece).

People are maturing. So It is logical for some human relationships to change, to evolve, and some to disappear for ever, and perhaps for this reason they were created from the beginning, to be lost. It is certain that nothing remains the same if we desire change.

The quality person who will move you forward and upgrade your life wants to see you happy, so he/she tries to produce enjoyable moments with you. He/she provides knowledge, does not tolerate mediocrity and is constantly upgraded!

With those you associate with, you will look like ...

How many of you have sacrificed a minute, an hour, a sunset, a day or a lifetime to be with people who pull you down? With tired, who murmur, who have no appetite, who talk negatively, who are pessimistic and constantly in distress ...

Get rid of these toxic people, and if you can't get rid of and cut the umbilical cord that connects you with them, make sure you spend as little time with them as possible!

With those you associate with, you will look like ...

The phrase: Those you associate with will resemble them, is authentic and apply in 100% of cases. And I'll ask you now, how many times have you sacrificed a smile, your happy mood, your joy, your silliness, your energy, your appetite, to share your feelings with a friend / relative / acquaintance who was tired , miserable, jealous, whining or complaining constantly?

And if you answer: "yes, I do it", "often", "many times", "almost daily", then another question will come up that will make you change your attitude: What do you offer to this person harmonizing and associate your own good psychology with misery, fatigue and negativity?

With those you associate with, you will look like ...

Do you offer something useful to the person you have opposite you? Are you helping him somewhere? Are you evolving as a human being? Will he get rid of his problem, or will he perpetuate it for ever? The answer is: NO! YOU OFFER ABSOLUTELE NOTHING ... Only he destroys you. With its toxicity, its constant tired mood and its misery, it pulls you to the mud!

This is for the following reason, because there is the support that compels you to pursue this self-destructive behavior in order to make the person you spend hours with and care about not feeling alone ...

Something that does not happen really, it will simply perpetuate a problem and the negative emotions will swell, because as we know, we cannot get rid of negative emotions if we blindfold or fail to recognize them!

With those you associate with, you will look like ...

Therefore, make sure you feel beautiful every day and nobody spoils your mood. Change the subject to something that is going to 'throw' you, not continue a conversation that hides dangers and spend time with quality people, that you have something to learn from them, something to take in order to transmit and to others, friends, children ... and so on.

Every beginning

As in all areas of our lives, so are businesses and more Real Estate field, the early stages

needed for a Real Estate Agent are:

Operating permission

Learn what is needed to get an operation permission & licence to practice profession (Depending on Country, City, Area)

Education & Examinations

☐ Be aware of the types of real estate contracts that in your area.

☐ Familiarize yourself with real estate terminology. There are many terms that apply namely real estate negotiations. Read widely about buying and selling process, to incorporate terms.

☐ Understand the tax laws and their tax implications are related to real estate.

☐ Be familiar with confidential relationships and obligations notification.

Partnerships with Registered Real Estate Agents (especially for young people) Real estate agents).
New real estate agents are usually required to work with a registered one real estate agent for a period of time to get the new one real estate agent experience and acquaintances to make it possible independent. As for the most experienced and experienced real estate agents, partnerships are the cornerstone of a common market, in an area where the needs are mutually fulfilled and a great sale is achieved.

Partnerships with Registered Real Estate Agents (especially for young Real estate agents).

New real estate agents are usually required to work with a registered one real estate agent for a period of time to get the new one real estate agent experience and acquaintances to make it possible independent. As for the most experienced with long experience experienced real estate agents, partnerships are the foundation stone of a common market, in an area where the needs are mutually fulfilled and a great sale is achieved.

Develop a contact list. The real estate sector is about who you know. Connecting to a wide network of people engaged either in investment or in the field of real estate, will help you in creating a significant number of new ones contacts.

☐ Use client management software to continue with the list your contacts so you don't forget any customers (previous customers, current or prospective buyers).

Create a website and get intence presence on social media.

Connect with people who are not in your immediate contact circle, communicating online, or through social media.

☐ Make social media sites dedicated to your business real estate sector.

☐ Tweet listings and tips for real estate like you you can present them.

☐ Follow what others say / do on social media to promote opportunities for new ones businesses.

☐ Post your lists and how others search real estate (such as links directing customers to specific properties, offers etc.).

☐ **Be a welcoming personality to everyone who you meet, but at the same time you are special personality.**

☐   "People may not remember what you did or what you you told them, but they will always remember how you did them feel »

A person posing for the camera

Description automatically generated

TOPIC SECTION "C"

Communication Techniques

Approching potential buyers

Contact with customers

COMMUNICATION TECHNIQUES

Your personality is strongly influenced by the people you interact with, so it is important to make your customers feel special, paying full attention while you are with them. Operate ALWAYS with two basic communication tactics:

☐ **Active Listening:** Learn to listen, it's one of the key elements in coaching. Listen with 4 ears say, hear 70% and talk 30% is the right ratio. To listen and be present, because ONLY so will you be able to understand and gain empathy, and another reason is confidence. When you do not interrupt and listen carefully, the customer will be even more open to you!

☐ **Empathy:** A word full of emotions and psychic reserves. Identifying emotions, deepening them, and understanding them fully so that you can experience the feelings that someone else is experiencing, originally had a Hellenistic word, the word empathy. Something that today we have naturally rejected and distorted as to the meaning and value of empathy with the utterly opposite meaning, hatred and dislike, antipathy.

EMPATHY

Lipps gives a definition in 1903 that empathy is the intrinsic side of imitation, also believing that it is the key force we can acquire as a human species.

And Rogers goes on to regard it as one of the "necessary and sufficient conditions for a therapeutic personality change."

We should be very aware that we cannot fully understand and penetrate a person's psychological macrocosm - and therefore identify with his feelings - if we rely solely on the verbal part of our communication.

EMPATHY

That is, if we rely only on words and not on "secret" messages that we can decrypt. **The key to empathy lies in the signs of nonverbal communication.** We should also know that only 7% is based on our verbal action in a dialogue, a meeting, a discussion or a speech, and the remaining 93% is based on nonverbal actions that can reveal everything, observing reactions of the person. Non-verbal elements of communication include body language (body movements, hands, posture, gait, gestures), facial expressions, and tone-of-voice.

One 'trap' that many may fall into trying to understand, understand and identify with is the loss of themselves! They lose a part of themselves, experiencing someone else's situation as their own. C. Rogers had stated that Empathy is an important point in life. **You have to get in the other's place but never forget the "as if it were me".** That is, to not completely identify with and lose your own piece and essence and then act in a way that is completely influenced and completely dependent on the feelings of the other, which you have done to yourself. Be careful never to forget the 'as if' ... As if you were in the position of the other and not the other! Empathy must be done in such a way that we can enter the place of another without losing the integrity of our being.

Empathy is the emotional identification with another person. The recognition and understanding of another person's position, emotion, thoughts. A person who uses empathy can recognize and feel what another person is feeling, so he / she can understand him / her better. In this way he / she can put himself in the position of the other and recognize his / her motivations, his / her concerns, and the behavior he /she has developed, and therefore the cause. That is, to see the world through his / her eyes. **It is a powerful communication tool.**

In order to achieve this connection, this bond, and the relationship with the other person, you need to have **consciousness control**.

Consciousness control as it requires to be present.

CONTACTING CUSTOMERS

"DO NOT HEAR WHO YOU WANT TO ANSWER BUT WHAT THE OTHER WANTS TO LEARN"

☐ Keep in touch with previous customers. 65-75% of real estate sales generally come from recommendations.

☐ Send a satisfaction gift to the customer after a successful sale.

☐ Call customers 1-2 months after closing to make sure they are satisfied and if they need some support.

☐ Send an annual Newsletter to all your previous clients.

CONTACTING CUSTOMERS

☐ Talk comfortably about buying, selling, about your beliefs about contracts and real estate, talk about and explain to people who are not familiar with the real estate market.

☐ Collaborate with new people to create new interfaces

☐ Listen to your customers and reach out to their needs.

☐ Attend local conferences and meetings.

☐ Grant to local schools and sports teams.

☐ Recommend yourself to your area.

CONTACTING CUSTOMERS

Keep in touch with real estate professionals. Building connections with people in the real estate industry gives you a network of professionals who will support each other. Keep your network strong by interacting with as many other brokers as you can.

☐ Participation in local events, clubs, Real Estate Agents.

- [ ] Get in touch with a mentor to ask questions and compare ideas.

- [ ] Use customer feedback to tailor your approach.

CONTACTING CUSTOMERS

- [ ] Observe market and region trends. As mentioned above, real estate markets are constantly changing. Be aware of the factors that affect pricing and availability in your area.

- [ ] Maintain a database in your area to find comparable prices.

- [ ] Keep track of the values and trends of residential areas.

A GOOD SELLER

A GOOD SELLER :

☐ **He should know how: People do not buy objects but identities! Emotion plays a dominant role**! Therefore, in order to be able to reach them and come to you, they need to know 100% that you understand them and that you are authentic in what you do. That you know exactly what they need and why.

☐ Clients need to feel that you can understand their problem in depth to help them.

☐ **The language you use should be attractive and understandable!** There should be words in your vocabulary like "Imagine", "Envisage", "Great" etc.

☐ Offer what the other wants to learn and not what you want to sell or promote. Do not drown your interlocutor with knowledge and words and a whole bunch of things that are not appropriate in the present situation, but confuse the person sitting opposite you and may even cancel a sale.

COMMUNICATION SKILLS

You should know that in a first contact-chat with your customer, you have:

4 minutes to reveal yourself and say who you are and what you do, what you provide. After the first 4 minutes, we form 90% of our view of the person we have against us.

Verbal communication only plays a role in 7%.

55% comes from facial expressions and body language

And 38% from non-verbal aspects of speech (volume, tone, tone, voice quality).

Physiology (our movements) directly affects our minds, that is, our thoughts and emotions.

 Therefore, you should listen carefully to your interlocutor and observe the movements he / she makes with his / her hands, body, facial expressions and physiology in general. If you are experienced enough, you may be able to observe and breathe, which is very important!

Page 43

COMMUNICATION MISTAKES

Some mistakes that you may need to avoid in a first look, a first contact with your interlocutor is:

A) Do not hunch, but keep your back firm. When you are hunching it is a message that you are "locked in", you get bored, you have no opinion on the subject, you have no capacity and you feel uncomfortable and pressured. And besides, fallen shoulders, bowing and turning back, raise the levels of the hormone cortisol, thus producing stress in your body.

Page 44

COMMUNICATION MISTAKES

B) When you nod too much or when you make excessive gestures.

The above is an indication that you are trying to convince someone in every way about your point of view and the truth (exaggerated gestures), or that you seem to agree and understand what you are hearing but without doing so (exaggerating).

Page 45

COMMUNICATION MISTAKES

C) Intense visual contact indicates aggression.

Ideally it would be 8 to 10 seconds to constantly focus on the eyes of your interlocutor, say the scientists. Take a short break and then focus again. On the contrary, of course, when we avoid visual contact, it automatically means that our words are unreliable. We do not have much confidence in what we say and it shows that we want to hide something. So balance is needed.

Page 46

COMMUNICATION MISTAKES

D) Hands in the waist ...

This movement works just like crossed arms and legs, as it shows that we are blocking the ideas of others. It is a sign of introversion and that we do not want dialogue indirectly.

COMMUNICATION MISTAKES

E) Looking at the clock,

playing with your hair, or with your collar, is a sign of impatience that you lack confidence and distract from the subject.

COMMUNICATION MISTAKES

G) Finally, the fake smile

it is easy to recognize and may cause trouble. People who know how to decode your facial expressions will perceive you immediately when you are truly laughing, or when you are pretending to be laughing. And this energy is obvious, because when you are genuinely smiling, your eyes also smile with your mouth (goose foot) and many of the facial muscles are activated, in opposition to the fake that focuses only on the mouth (lips).

TOPIC SECTION "D"

The role of the R.A.S in achieving targets

Seller vs Buyer goals

TARGETS

 # 1: What do you really want to achieve this year? For many people, this question often leads to three answers: money, health and relationships. But regardless of your answer, I want **you go deep and answer specifically the following questions (Coaching):**

☐　　Why is there any obstacle to you (whatever the issue that keeps you constantly in doubt and fear)?

☐　　What do the goals mean to you?

☐　　Does your goal motivate you?

☐ The big "WHY". Why do you want to achieve that goal? What is its essence?

TARGETS

2: What new skills / procedures and routines are needed to achieve your goals?

That has brought you into a situation similar to the one you lived in or the backwaters and downhills, it is certain that it cannot get you where you want it, that is, to rise and succeed. So you change your daily routine, your routine, and you deal with the things that help you reach your goal, not the ones that drive you away. You change activities and habits that you did until yesterday.

☐ Think... What do you need to change?

☐ A new mentality perhaps?

☐ A new set of skills?

☐ What skills will create the "bridge" to reach your goal?

Adopt new mindsets / habits / hobbies or develop those skills that you see as needing development. Get new skills. If it's not in your schedule, and if you don't commit to it, it's not going to happen!

TARGETS

 # 3: What Old Beliefs, Habits, or Practices Is It Time to Leave Behind?

☐   Self-analysis and awareness!

"I've done everything" you will say to yourself, trying to convince him ... Maybe not? Are there any limiting beliefs that sabotage you?

Ask yourself what you need to leave behind to improve (yourself).

☐   What do you need to recognize?

☐   What anchors hold the boat down to the sea floor?

☐   What thoughts do you need to leave behind to move forward and not sink?

☐   Reduce Negative Thoughts?

☐   Negative and Counterproductive Beliefs?

☐   Drainage of vitality and passion?

☐   Inadequate procedures?

☐   Habits / Hobbies / Routines that do not help evolution?

☐   **TARGETS**

What are the best tips for business planning and life planning?

The most important step in successful planning is to realize that life is a marathon not a sprint.

And here's the paradox:

People tend to overestimate what they can achieve in a year, but they dramatically underestimate what they can achieve in five years!

The problem is that everyone is looking for success unconditionally, easily and quickly. The vast majority of people have no patience. They are willing to exert a lot of energy in short bursts, but lose momentum in the long run.

ENVISAGE

One great exercise to overcome this is **to develop a truly long-term view of your life**: Imagine yourself in ten years from today and describe your entire life in specific details.

- ☐ How would you like your lifestyle to look like?
- ☐ What habits do you have in your daily life?
- ☐ How do you feel?
- ☐ How do you wake up?
- ☐ Where are you?
- ☐ What do you eat?
- ☐ How do you get to the office?

Try to experience success as it does now, right now! Use all your senses. What do you see around you? What do you hear? What sounds do you get in your ears? How do you feel physically?
VISUALIZATION

- ☐ And coming to the present, what actions are needed to achieve what you have just dreamed of

TARGETS

☐   When you have a vision of where you are going in life, **you are better prepared to withstand and overcome the inevitable challenges you** will encounter while traveling.

☐   **Stay unswerving,** without distractions. With a plan in place, you become more assertive.

☐   **Create your own plan** and follow it with confidence to create the future you want.

The space in REAL ESTATE The real estate field is wide and constantly changing, so you need to be properly prepared.

Americans say "**Start your Database YESTERDAY**!" and they are absolutely right! You need to create a database of existing customers, what they are asking (where and how), even in some cases when there are alternatives, the "game" comes in and the question "why?" Why do you need this property in this area? This part etc ... The Database list will also include previous clients of course in the archive, with names, contact details, residence area, even ages! It's like building your own skyscraper, step-by-step, floor-to-floor ...

START YOUR DATABASE YESTERDAY!

SELL YOURSELF

Sell yourself! It is more important than just selling a property. As a Broker / Agent, knowing how to "sell" yourself requires insistence and patience. Get involved in your work circles, get involved in events, get training in your field, keep in touch with people in the same area, and slowly build yourself up.

You are building today what you are going to sell tomorrow, and this is what everybody wants to buy ...

Dynamics, Confidence, Personality, Security!

As I said before, maintain your relationship with your customer! Communication and contact is an important part of a Real Estate Agent, both on a personal level and on new horizons that open up for him. The **SUCCESSFUL** Real Estate Agent is based on Communication!

A frequent mistake ...

One major mistake that 99% of Real Estate Agents make and lose customer communication is the answer to the Question:

How is the market? 99% responds like: Bad or good, or I'm good / we are doing well, the situation is going to get better, nothing is moving, costs are coming up, it's difficult, and so much more. At this point all communication is lost completely. To be able the dialogue to continue, the customer's "attraction", the correct answer is: **DEPENDS**!

Page 59

TOM FERRY

The Real Estate Market Situation Depends on many factors,
according to

1 Real Estate Coach Tom Ferry.

It depends on:

☐ **The area**. Other areas are always moving less and others more.

☐ **The budget / amount.** A property with a value of A when it acquires a value of B is expected to sell sooner. Usually (even in a strong crisis in the construction sector), as prices go down, sales or rent increase.

☐ **Buy or Rent?** Do you want to rent? Do you want to sell? IT DEPENDS!

☐ **Is it a plot, a house, an apartment, an investment**? THEY ALL DEPEND ON A WIDE VARIETY OF FACTORS!

IT DEPENDS

A great deal on the question "how is the market?" and on the clever answer to "**IT DEPENDS**", is the connection / building a client relationship with a real estate agent. Instead of a lazy and weak 'What to do, what everybody is doing' or 'Something is going to be done', an interesting discussion can take place, where you learn information about a prospective buyer or investor, and you can offer your knowledge and your experience analyzing the market with the famous word "**IT DEPENDS ...**"

HANDSHAKES

Another thing to keep in mind when meeting a new person, going for a first interview in order to hire you, or when making a new acquaintance, is handshake. The types of handshakes vary. Here, I'm going to reveal the basics for you to be well prepared before you lend yourself a few seconds to the person you come into contact with.

A) A firm and confident handshake is more or less predictable and expected, but it is a good starting point, especially in the work environment and showing good will.

B) Handshake with trembling hands, indicates anxiety and fear.

C) Handshake on the fingertips indicates uncertainty, cautiousness and courtesy.

D) Handshake, shaking hands up and down, indicates an extroverted and expressive person.

E) Handshake with one hand while the other rests on the shoulder of the interlocutor. This person wants to show superiority, even pride. Sign of selfishness.

G) Handshake with two hands (sandwich). It means modesty, that he is a prudent person. Often, it also shows a confident person.

DISTANCES

Another communication tip you should follow is the distance you keep from your interlocutor.

The following zones will give you a field, and how to move according to the circumstances: **A) The familiar zone.** In the familiar zone we usually keep a distance of half a meter (at most). Our parents, our children, and our family in general are in the zone.

B) The personal belt, is usually half a meter long and can extend up to one meter and thirty centimeters (approx.). In this zone is the distance we hold in events, gatherings, friendly gatherings. □

C) The social zone ranges from approximately one and a half meters and extends to three and a half meters (approx.). In this zone, we place people we don't know well. Either from our work environment or from a craftsman who has come to our home.

D) The public zone. In this zone we address the public when we give a lecture, or when we address a large group of people, and the distance we have to keep is over three and a half meters.

THE MAGIC QUESTION

What is the magic question to ask a buyer the first time you talk to them on the phone? Quite simply: THERE IS NO MAGIC QUESTION! Just stop creating scripts and hypotheses for your customers. We have seen clients who seem to be 'incompetent' buyers and prove to be strong investors, as well as fewer easy-to-raise customers who want an expensive property, who are presented with expensive cars and clothes and ultimately fail get the coveted bank loan. **Think about what this person really needs** instead of looking for some kind of "magic" question or speculation.

How Can I Overcome the Fear of Success?

When someone says they have a fear of success, they often hide the fear of something else. Success itself does not scare most people, what it scares, as I find out through the sessions, is the fear of loneliness, change, risk, success, in the sense that "too much money destroys people" that is clearly another unpleasant and restrictive belief held by some deep within them. It's the many hours, the sweat, the rejection, the vulnerability - it's **all the WORK needed for the success** that usually scares people.

THE MONEY ARE NOT RESPONSIBLE

"MONEY DOES NOT DESTROY HUMAN, HIS VALUES DESTROY"

A person who has a capable and positive system of values, likes to offer, likes to share love, to help people, with success and money, his / her values will be **REINFORCED**. One who, being a miser, does not believe in human relations, lacks empathy and sensitivity, his / her success will be simply SWEELED UP. **It is purely a matter of VALUES & WISHES and NOT money!**

SUCCESS

Success in real estate starts with the reality that concerns you. If you are willing to endure and work hard and fight, then this path will lead to growth. If you don't want to do the hard work every day, not tire out, not try and but wait for ready-made customers, then this might not be the right job for you.

The fear of failure is also very unpleasant. You will not be able to pay your expenses, what it is built, you see it collapse, you see your money in bank accounts going down and you feel like a failure ... NO!

R.A.S. and NEUROPLASTICITY

RID OF DISASTER SCENARIOS !

"After one has succeeded, everyone can!"

And here, we will talk scientifically about WHAT YOU CAN DO!

Our reality listens to the name R.A.S..

When there is a ruminant of negative thoughts and bad scenarios, our brain and the "R.A.S. system" cannot perceive them as mere thoughts, and incorporate them into your subconscious, considering them as real! Therefore, your brain and your subconscious will do WHAT is possible to prove that what you think is true!

R.A.S. and NEUROPLASTICITY

Positive Thoughts and Positive Statements.

Let me explain briefly the law of attraction from its scientific point of view.

The **RAS = Reticular Activating System,** commonly called the Network Activation System, is that part of the brain (at its base) that passes all the billions of information and stimuli we receive from the outside world (outside us, extrinsic factors), that is, our whole daily life, our day, our week, our month, our time, **our whole life**!

R.A.S. and NEUROPLASTICITY

Now, let's talk about the role of RAS. The RAS section acts as a selector, as a bus, so it "unrolls" it as useless and unnecessary. Through RAS passes all this information and stimuli we receive daily, however, of the billions of information, **ONLY 2,000 to 3,000 RAS lets pass to our brain** !!! It is unthinkable and yet real! Only a few thousands of stimuli and information allow us to reach out and define our lives. The important thing, of course, is not this, but **WHY** does it remove and eliminate all the "useless" information and stimuli we receive?

R.A.S. and NEUROPLASTICITY

RAS allows information to enter the brain for two main reasons:

SURVIVAL. It allows us to access information that is necessary and useful for our survival. What we need to live (food, water, breaths, heartbeats, etc.).

FOCUSING. GATHERS INFORMATION THAT CONSIDERS IMPORTANT FOR US! TO WHAT WE FOCUS AND TO WHAT WE CONCENTRATE ON! Therefore, if our thoughts are negative, unpleasant, pessimistic, the part of the RAS brain will leave information and stimuli to create our lives based on the thoughts we do and the focus on. That is, you will live and absorb everything that has to do with pessimism and negativity. But if our thoughts are positive, optimistic, focused on success and goal-setting strategies, this will also be the information and stimuli we receive daily and allow RAS to take root in our subconscious to create our reality!

COMMITMENT

60% - 70% of real estate agents fail before reaching the five year real estate market. The first step to your success is to **make the commitment** to do whatever it takes to survive in the long run. Listen to what you need, observe what you need to observe, DO WHAT YOU SAY NECESSARY to achieve your goal. **Answer "Why?"**

COMMITMENT

Identifying your motivations is the next essential step on the road to success. Why do you want to achieve this goal, why? **Building a successful Real Estate business means taking on the role and responsibilities of being the CEO of your own business.** It's a huge commitment.

Real Estate Is Not a "haphazardly" job.

Success in real estate is never a «fast food». It is not a harp and glue without patience. You are going to do today the things that will create a prosperous future.

TALK MORE

Bill Mitchell had said, "Never hunt for money! **Success is to become the kind of person who offers so much value in the market that money follows him**. "Your income is directly related to the value you deliver. And that requires patience, perseverance, strategy and plan. Out there on the World Market there are people who are paid 3 euros an hour and 50 euros an hour, even at 100 € / hour, 200 € / hour and 1,000 and many more (YES!). It is the value they give to the market, not the hours they work. **UPGRADE YOUR VALUE**!

Talk to people every day.

At the end of the day, real estate can be a business. **Whoever talks to most people wins**. Make sure you talk to people everyday. Give them value. Ask them if they need any help or support. The biggest reason brokers fail is because they do not talk to anyone and are simply "locked" in an office, expecting a coveted phone ringer or a passing customer.

Page 74

THE 3 QUESTIONS

☐   **3 questions to ask yourself about your business:**

☐   **1. What exactly am I committed to doing this year? You can't hunt two rabbits at a time, says the proverb** ...

You need to focus on what you want **and focus all your attention on it!**

☐   **2. What ritual attitudes should there be**?

What are the things you are going to do every day, **even when you don't want to?**

These are the actions that will give you **the strength to persevere** in difficult times. These daily habits, daily little actions, actions (hobbies as I mentioned above) that will put you on the path to growth.

☐ **3. What are the systemic changes needed to maintain the new levels of growth?**

If you have a lot of development growth, but you don't have the system in place, it won't work ... That means you work more hours to try and prevent it from happening.

WOULD YOU LIKE TO SUCCEED?

Robin Sharma reports how only 5% of all businesses succeed because 95% think the same way. Those who plan plans, plan a strategy towards a goal, are just 5%.

"Do you want to succeed? Think differently! "

REALISTIC OBJECTIVES

Well, sometimes we have to do it for ourselves. Do not «walk on the clouds »! Many real estate agents and businessmen stick around before starting the big step, setting unrealistic goals. This results in setbacks and high frustration, due to unexpected situations that they will be called upon to deal with, they will blame on others, create a bad and unpleasant climate, a dysfunctional environment, and come to swamp!

If you put 1000kg of pressure on yourself to make some great achievements, but you don't put in the solid foundations to get there, you will never succeed.

REALISTIC OBJECTIVES

Realistic and Attainable Goals! Know your capabilities, your abilities and move on to those levels. If you want to upgrade your skills and enhance your abilities, you **CAN** do it with a plan and with continuous training.

You need a plan, a strategy. Step-by-step you go up the ladder and do not jump with a jump to the highest step! Set basic goals first. The least you can produce. A small number of sales / operations that will ensure your viability. Then set bigger goals. "Break" is a big goal in everyday wins.

THE PERSPECTIVE

It's time to adjust your perception. How many of the challenges you face are real and how many do you perceive differently? **Research has shown that 80% of situations we fear will happen ... NEVER HAPPEN!**

Don't exaggerate a problem. Don't overemphasize something negative that happened. If you change the way you see the world, the world around you will start to change.

SELLER - BUYER

There is obviously a big gap between buyers and sellers and you have to bridge it. **Keep a balance between Owner and Buyer** so you don't 'throw' each other in the other's eyes and instantly destroy the sale.

Do you negotiate with your customers? Are you discussing? Do you answer their questions? Do you understand their needs?

Have you found the point of mutual acceptance between them? Find out what themes and points a buyer and seller agree on and emphasize there. Don't take the negative points and any tensions as badly and tastelessly to the other side as the results will be unpleasant and you will most likely not finish the transaction.

Page 80

SELLER - BUYER

Win buyers and owners alike. Gain confidence and intimacy. To do this, some useful questions to ask are:

What will happen if you buy / sell your home? What will you gain, what will change in your life?

What will happen if you don't?

What will not happen if you do?

What will not happen if you don't buy?

Have you considered all the options A, B, C...?

Also ask if the buyer has a family or is he alone so you can guide him. If you like crowds, strolls, a walk in the city, or if you prefer nature, the wind of a suburb, or a village.

Which restaurants he prefers, where does he come from, if he needs to find a property near Airport, Port, Hospital, School ...

Whether it's a modern type, modern, or more classic.

 ALL OF THE ABOVE WILL PLAY A MAJOR ROLE IN YOUR RELATIONSHIP WITH THE BUYER AND YOU WILL UNDERSTAND THEIR NEEDS AND PERSONALITY!

TOPIC SECTION "E"

What is Sales

Sales Techniques

Good Salesman Skills

Teamwork

Dynamic Questions

SALES

☐ **Identify** and understand the needs of your buyers.

☐ **Use** a measurable, repetitive Sales Process that you can evaluate if it succeeds.

☐ **Know your product** very well.

☐ **Practical active listening.**

☐ Learn to manage your emotions. Do not fall into the trap, for example if you meet an eccentric buyer or landlord, or an aristocratic, full of conceit and arrogance and flood you with feelings of injustice, revenge, anger and rage that will lead to a provocative response and quarrel.

Manage your emotions and respond in a beautiful way.

SALES

Believe in what you are selling!

Identify your strongest motivation. What drives you to success?

View customer success as yours. Rejoice with the sale as if it were your own piece. Part of your life (that is).

Build personal relationships.

Prepare on time. NOT at the last minute. The stress you make will make you more aggressive, more distant, and more nonchalant. Be prepared for **a meeting without ANXIETY and stress.**

Look for potential customers wherever you go. You never know you will meet a prospective buyer, an investor, a man who wants to change his life. It's everywhere, it's between us!

How to be a good sales representative and sell successfully:

Start with your goals.

If you are learning to sell, measuring your performance is the most important place to start.

☐ **How many clients** do you or your company need and on what schedule? (It is analyzed in the business plan at the end of the book).

☐ **How many salespersons** do you need to close a good number of customers (sales)?

☐ **How many interconnections** do you need and who will support you to discover new opportunities?

Make sure you set personal sales goals for both the CEO and the salespeople.

Recognize that sales are a process.

Sales are everywhere. In our lives, in our relationship with our partner, between the child and the parents: "Father. I want to go to London to do a doctorate "," But my child is a little bit dangerous there, he is away, plus it's a lot of money! "Mom replies. The child is trying to convince his parents, that a doctorate is a steppingstone for his life, an experience, it is his future.

So he is trying to sell - to convince his parents that he is something great. **It is a kind of sale, without necessarily direct economic activity.**

SALES

When you sell yourself, either in the business or hiring a company, you essentially sell: **Knowledge, Promise, Trust, Skills, Experience, Courtesy, Relationship Development, Good Mood, Service, Communication, Sympathy**!

Sales are an art many say. It's not just art. **Sales is a science**.

Sales are changing rapidly, but some things will stay the same. To get customers, you need to identify their needs and interest in your product, tackle inactivity in their business, and set a timetable for the sale.

The way your company is moving should be unique. **That is, you can outperform in many (if not all) of the above.**

If you treat every sales process in exactly the same way with each customer, in each business, you may lose several sales. So before you take the phone in hand with a purpose, be sure that you fully understand the process that your business operates. How it works, what activities it undertakes, what it provides, what solutions it can offer, **WHAT** will help the customer (buyer), and **WHY** to get the product from you and not from anyone else?

This will include **learning / strategy / marketing** of how to place your product and market it. Get strategies to talk to prospects, understand key value propositions, and find out **WHO** you are targeting in order to have a successful sales process.

Measure each step.

Anything worth doing is worth incorporating into your program and measuring it, and anything that can fit into your program can be improved to measure whether it's worth it!

Remember when setting your goals: Be faithful in measuring your sales performance. At the rate you're selling today, will you hit the numbers you want to reach by the end of the month or year? Do closure strategies allow new prospects for customers? If not, change something immediately.

Sell to people who want to buy.

This principle is at the heart of the inbound sales methodology.

This is the power of inbound marketing. Creating or restoring high quality and useful content and attracting prospects will save time and increase your chances of closing sales.

 The secret to being a successful sales professional is created by your long-standing relationship with your customers. **Every customer is different, so you need to tailor your approach to each individual's needs.** However, the building blocks of successful relationships do not change.

GOOD SALESPERSON'S BASIC ELEMENTS

☐ **Get to know your product,** including its features, capabilities and shortcomings. Get to know its advantages and disadvantages compared to similar products offered by the competition.

☐ **Good ways.** Always treat your prospective client with courtesy and respect, even if the client is annoying or has repeated questions, do not interrupt the client. **Active hearing!**

☐ **Curiosity is one of DaVinci's 7 principles of intelligence.** Learn as much from the customer as possible. The prospect and potential need for your product or service to get more information about the terms in which the product will be used. And this is achieved through dynamic questions! **Ask as many as you can to elicit all the answers you want to get and strengthen your relationship with trust!**

SALES

☐ **Do not calumniate competitors.** You need to be able to present the ways in which your product is superior, but do so **without vilifying another product**, or worse, another competitor person or company. The customer will most likely not appreciate some bad reviews that you will say about a product competing with yours for many reasons. One of the main ones is to consider you an arrogant and a superficial person. Also another reason is that the customer may be a supporter of other products, something you immediately disregard by misrepresenting it. You may also think that you are overbearing and immediately «fall in his / her eyes» prey to your product, or even he / she knows people who work in other businesses (competing with yours) and refute your reason.

Flexibility. How can you help the customer make the best possible purchase? Be flexible and move according to the needs of the customer and not with the object (or service) you want to place.

Leave your mark. A card, a promotion, a presentation, a CD, and even an email with your company's products and services. Make the customer remember you!

Communication. If the sale succeeds, contact the customer in a few weeks or months to see if he or she is happy. And if not, find out why and do something to resolve that discontent.

Buyer categories are divided into:

A. Those who are unhappy with the products of a business.

B. Those who are simply satisfied with the products of a business.

C. Those who are excited about a company's products.

Page 94

SALES

In the first category, you do not want to be **and you must NOT be**.

In the second category, you just go indifferent. If you lack all of these features I mentioned earlier (Knowledge, Promise, Confidence, Skills, Experience, Courtesy, Relationship Development, Good Mood, Service, Communication, Sympathy!) You may pass unnoticed, without personality, among thousands just "pass" a customer on your way, and tomorrow may not come again.

☐ **In the third category IT IS NECESSARY to be**! Because they are superior to almost all of the above, and most importantly to Trust, service and knowledge.

TEAMWORK

You are a part of a team, whether you're the CEO, the HR Manager, the Business Owner, the Real Estate Agent, or the Salesperson! The group consists of: "two or more individuals interacting in such a way that each is influences and is influenced by the other" (Moorhead and Griffin, 1998). The dynamics of the team are shaped by exactly this **interaction**, as well as with everything that happens during the operation of the team, such as agreed rules, roles being developed and all communication

TEAMWORK

Diversity within the group, in terms of opinions, opinions, knowledge and skills, is not necessary! That is to say, there is no need for all members of a team to agree on everything and with everything, **ON THE CONTRARY**!

Diversity in opinions and knowledge enables the team to evolve, produce a creative dialogue and examine all possible perspectives before making the final decisions.

TEAMWORK / FEATURES

Clearly, not all groups are equally effective. There are, however, some groups of traits that bring the desired results and achieve their goals. These are:

☐ **To have strong core values** that its members have established for the way they operate and the goals they pursue.

☐ **To Have a general purpose conversion into specific and clear**, objective goals as well as positive feedback on performance.

☐ **The contribution of the members should be considered necessary,** unique and evaluated against specific and previously known criteria.

(Schermerhorn)

TEAMWORK / FEATURES

To be able to be part of a group, or to be able to lead a group and create a group, you need to know the characteristics of the group:

1. Every person, like every piece of the puzzle, is unique and without it you will not be come the desired result.

2. We set boundaries. Personal boundaries, professional boundaries, boundaries that allow us to move within the group.

3. Define roles in a group. What is the **SPECIFIC** and **CLEAR** role of each member.

4. Some pieces of the puzzle play a central role and other pieces are supportive, **BUT they all need** for a successful result!

5. Incentives. There must be motivation within the group to mobilize and move into action.

6. Each team member is as unique as any human being on earth!

TEAMWORK / FEATURES

Collaboration between parties in a group is the STRONG point... (it should)

- ☐ **Exist collaboration** and sharing of knowledge and information with other members

- ☐ **Have a team spirit**

- ☐ **Do not huddle up especially with the support of the team leader**

- ☐ **Skills & Capacity reinforcement**

- ☐ **Exist Conflict management between parties**. Learn team members to resolve any differences and manage tensions and conflicts.

- ☐ **Have Good communication and respect.** Team should work in a beautiful and functional environment.

- ☐ **Celebrate and reward a team with its wins!**

Page 100

FORBES – ADVICES

Finally, some tips given by Real Estate Agents through Forbes Magazine:

- ☐ **DON'T SELL...** Our first responsibility is not to sell but to do Coaching to the client. Build a relationship and understand customer needs. What he / she really needs!

- ☐ **When you create VALUES.** Value for yourself and value to the customer, you increase confidence!

- ☐ **Honesty!** If you want good reputation, you have to be moral and honest!

- ☐ **Offer choices** and not be absolute!

- ☐ **Continuous education** and information in the field of Real Estate!

- ☐ **Be willing to help**, kindly and respectfully!

- ☐ Active listening. Listen to understand!

- ☐ **Don't go unnoticed**. Create a business that is constantly active (events, media, social media).

- ☐ **Communication and action**. Do not rest, take action!

BUSINESS COACHING (FREQUENT) QUESTIONS

- ☐ What's working right now?

- ☐ What doesn't work?

- ☐ Where are you and where would you like to go the company?

- ☐ What do you expect to achieve this year, given the plans and strategies you have implemented?

- ☐ What are the positive results you are committed to producing?

- ☐ What are the challenges and obstacles your business faces?

- ☐ What are the priority areas where your business could benefit most from coaching?

BUSINESS COACHING (FREQUENT) QUESTIONS

- ☐ What goal do you want to achieve?
- ☐ What do you really want (from your inner)?
- ☐ What would you like to accomplish?
- ☐ What result are you trying to achieve?
- ☐ What result would be ideal?
- ☐ What do you want to change?
- ☐ WHY do you hope to achieve this goal?
- ☐ What would be the benefits of achieving this goal?

Page 103

BUSINESS COACHING (FREQUENT) QUESTIONS

What are your choices?

What do you think you should do next?

What would be your first step?

What do you think you need to do to get a better result (or get closer to your goal)?

Who else could help?

What will happen if you do nothing?

What has already worked for you?

How could you do more than that?

What if you did this?

What is the hardest part for you?

What is the best / worst thing with this choice?

What could you do differently?

NOTE: Not all questions are suitable for all people. Here are some useful and helpful questions and the Real Estate Coach (Life & Business Coach) should use them on a case-by-case basis.

www.ingramcontent.com/pod-product-compliance
Lightning Source LLC
Chambersburg PA
CBHW020617220526
45463CB00006B/2608